Exploring Australia

Using Charts, Graphs, and Tables

Holly Cefrey

PowerMath™

New Hanover County Public Library
201 Chestnut Street
Wilmington, NC 28401

Published in 2004 by The Rosen Publishing Group, Inc.
29 East 21st Street, New York, NY 10010

Copyright © 2004 by The Rosen Publishing Group, Inc.

Book Design: Michael J. Flynn

Photo Credits: Cover © David Lawrence/Corbis; p. 7 © Danny Lehman/Corbis; p. 9 © L. Clarke/Corbis;
p. 14 © Royalty-Free/Corbis; p. 15 © Paul A. Souders/Corbis; p. 16 © Eric and David Hosking/Corbis;
p. 18 © Brian A. Vikander/Corbis; p. 19 © Tony Arruza/Corbis; p. 21 (Great Barrier Reef) © Peter Walton/
Index Stock; p. 21 (clam) © Stephen Frink/Corbis; p. 22 © Fred Kamphues/SuperStock.

Library of Congress Cataloging-in-Publication Data

Cefrey, Holly.
  Exploring Australia : using charts, graphs, and tables / Holly Cefrey.

      v. cm. - (PowerMath)
Includes index.
Contents: Let's explore Australia - Sunny days - The land of Australia
- The people of Australia - Aussie wildlife - A very big rock.
  ISBN 0-8239-8969-0 (lib. bdg.)
  ISBN 0-8239-8883-X (pbk.)
  6-pack ISBN: 0-8239-7392-1
  1. Graphic methods-Juvenile literature. 2. Australia-Juvenile
literature. [1. Graphic methods. 2. Australia-Description and travel.]
I. Title. II. Series.
  QA90.C44 2004
  001.4'226—dc21
    SNS   2003006022

Manufactured in the United States of America

Contents

Let's Explore Australia

Australia is a country and a **continent** that is entirely south of the **equator**. The name "Australia" comes from the Latin word "*australis,*" which means "southern." Anything south of the equator is part of the Southern **Hemisphere**. The United States is in the Northern Hemisphere. The seasons in the Southern Hemisphere are opposite of those in the Northern Hemisphere. When it is winter in the Northern Hemisphere, it is summer in the Southern Hemisphere.

Let's explore Australia by using tables, charts, and graphs. Tables show us different bits of information that are often organized in **columns** and rows. Charts and graphs show us information, too. Charts and graphs use shapes and colors to help us understand the information they show us.

This table shows the sizes of the 7 continents. Use the table to compare Australia to the other continents.

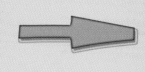

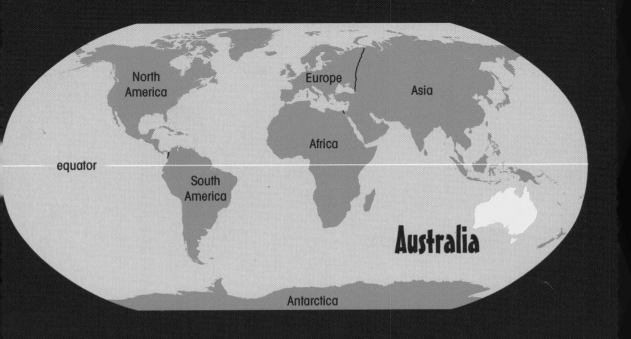

The 7 Continents

Continents	Land Size	
Asia	16,992,000 sq. mi.	44,008,000 sq. km.
Africa	11,657,000 sq. mi.	30,190,000 sq. km.
North America	9,347,000 sq. mi.	24,208,000 sq. km.
South America	6,889,000 sq. mi.	17,868,000 sq. km.
Antarctica	5,400,000 sq. mi.	14,000,000 sq. km.
Europe	4,015,000 sq. mi.	10,398,000 sq. km.
Australia	2,978,147 sq. mi.	7,713,364 sq. km.

Australia's official name is the **Commonwealth** of Australia. Australia is both a country and a continent. Australia is the sixth largest country in the world. It is also the smallest continent. Australia is known as the "island continent" because it is completely surrounded by water, just like an island. The Pacific Ocean is on the eastern coast. The Indian Ocean is on the western and southwestern coasts. The Coral and Timor Seas are on the northern coast. The Tasman Sea is on the southeastern coast.

Smaller neighboring islands are also a part of Australia. Tasmania, with an area of 26,000 square miles (67,800 square kilometers), is the largest island and the smallest of Australia's 6 states. The smallest Australian islands are little more than very large rocks.

This is a bar graph. The bars show the sizes of some of Australia's islands. There are thousands of islands that form part of Australia. This graph shows the 6 largest islands after Tasmania. Which is the largest island? Which is the smallest?

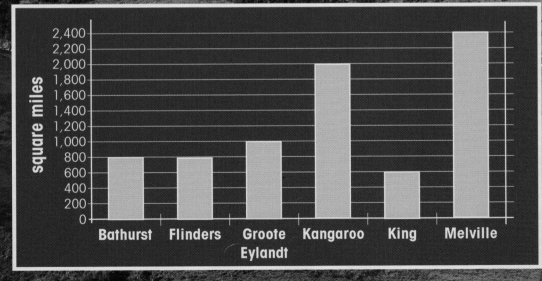

Australian Islands

square miles

Bathurst	Flinders	Groote Eylandt	Kangaroo	King	Melville

2,400 · 2,200 · 2,000 · 1,800 · 1,600 · 1,400 · 1,200 · 1,000 · 800 · 600 · 400 · 200 · 0

7

The northern part of Australia has tropical weather. It is mostly warm or hot and has a rainy season that lasts from November to April. The rest of the country has warm summers and cool winters. Snow falls only in Tasmania and in the Australian Alps, a mountain range in southeast Australia.

About $\frac{1}{3}$ of Australia is covered with desert, which makes up much of the central and western area of the country. Less than 10 inches (25 centimeters) of rain falls in the Australian desert each year, which makes it too dry to farm or raise livestock there. The northeastern coast receives the greatest amount of rainfall. It can rain as much as 150 inches (381 centimeters) a year there.

This map shows how much rain falls on the different areas of Australia. Below the map is a key that explains the different shades on the map. The color red shows which areas receive the most rainfall.

Rainfall in Australia

key		
color	**inches**	**centimeters**
	over 63	over 160
	47 to 63	120 to 160
	31 to 47	80 to 120
	16 to 31	40 to 80
	9 to 16	20 to 40
	under 9	under 20

The Land of Australia

Australia has 3 main land areas: the Eastern Highlands, the Central Lowlands, and the Western **Plateau**. The Eastern Highlands have sandy beaches, rocky cliffs, forests, rivers, plains, and the country's highest mountains. The Central Lowlands have farmland, grazing land for cattle, sandy deserts, and the lowest land in the country. The Western Plateau has deserts, grazing land for cattle, and low mountains.

The cattle, wheat, wool, dairy products, fruits, and sugarcane produced in Australia's farmlands provide an important source of the country's wealth. The nation's mineral resources provide another important source. Copper, gold, lead, silver, tin, zinc, coal, iron ore, natural gas, nickel, diamonds, and oil are all mined in Australia and exported to countries around the world. Most of Australia's manufacturing depends on the products that come from the country's farming and mining.

The 3 Main Land Areas of Australia

Area	Eastern Highlands	Central Lowlands	Western Plateau
Where	• eastern coast of the country	• west of the Eastern Highlands	• western $\frac{1}{3}$ of the country
Main Features	• highest land, mountain ranges • gets the most rain • many short rivers • mountains, forests, hills, rocky cliffs, plateaus, plains • excellent flat land for farming crops • rich, wet soils for crops	• lowest land (mostly low, flat) • gets the least rain • rivers during occasional rains; lakes that dry up • middle is desert • some areas with dry grasses and shrubs • much of the land is used for livestock grazing • some farming in the south	• mostly flat land, but higher than Lowlands • more rain than Lowlands • lakes and rivers • middle is desert • low mountain ranges • cattle raised on dry plains • some farming in northern and southwestern parts
People	• More than 9,000,000 people live between Brisbane and Melbourne.	• This area's largest cities have fewer than 30,000 people.	• Perth has about 2,000,000 people.

This table gives information about the 3 main land areas of Australia. You can use this table to answer questions about Australia. Which land area has the lowest lands? Which area gets the most rain? In which area would you find the city of Perth?

The People of Australia

The earliest Australians were **Aborigines**, who first arrived in Australia more than 65,000 years ago. Today, Aborigines form only a small part of Australia's population.

In 1605, a Dutch explorer named William Janszoon became the first European to reach Australia. In 1700, an Englishman named James Cook explored Australia's eastern coast. The first English people to settle there arrived In 1788, when England began to use Australia as a prison colony. The first group of prisoners founded the city of Sydney on Australia's southeastern coast.

Population of Australia

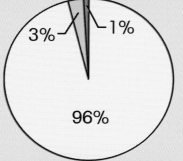

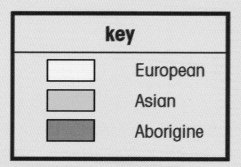

key

	European
	Asian
	Aborigine

This is a pie chart. Each slice of a pie chart stands for a certain amount of something. A large slice means that there is a lot. A small slice means that there is a little. This pie chart gives us information about the population of Australia.

Today, Australia's official language is English. However, Australian English is different from American English. Australians have some unusual words with their own special meanings. For example, "G'day, mate" (guh-DAY MAYT) is a greeting that means "Hello, friend." Other words, such as "kangaroo" and "koala," have been adopted from Aboriginal languages. The table on this page shows other special Australian words and their meanings.

Australian word	meaning
matilda	rolled-up blanket
brumbies	wild horses
dunny	toilet
ripper	great
squatters	owners of large farms
mob	herd of animals
bush	countryside

More than 80% of all Australians live in cities and towns. Most Aborigines also live in cities or towns. Most of Australia's cities are on or near the southeastern coast. This is where the largest cities—Melbourne and Sydney—can be found.

Very few people live in the middle of Australia or in the countryside. Only about 15% of Australians live in the country. Australians call the country the "bush." When you go far into the country, it is called the "outback." There are very few paved roads in the outback. Some people in the outback use small planes for easy and fast **transportation**.

Sydney

The map of Australia on page 15 shows how many people live in the different parts of Australia.
The color red shows where there are the most people per square mile (square kilometer). The color green shows where there are the fewest.

Population in Australia

Sydney

Melbourne

color	persons per square mile	persons per square kilometer
key		
	more than 10	more than 4
	5 to 10	2 to 4
	2 to 5	1 to 2
	fewer than 2	fewer than 1

outback

Aussie Wildlife

     Australia is home to some very special animals. These animals are native to Australia and are found in the wild only there. They include kangaroos, koalas, wallabies, wombats, and **platypuses**.

     Australia is home to some of the deadliest snakes in the world. These snakes include the tiger snake and the taipan. There are about 140 kinds of snakes, and most of them are poisonous. There are about 370 different kinds of lizards, none of which are poisonous.

     More than 700 kinds of birds are native to Australia. These include the black swan, the emu, and the kookaburra.

dingo

You can use this table to learn about some of the animals of Australia. Which of the animals on the table is the largest? Which is the smallest? Which animals on this table hatch from eggs?

Australia's Amazing Animals

	Where Found	What It Eats	Maximum Size	Activity	Babies
Wombat	coastal forests and grassy plains (Australia and Tasmania)	grass, bushes, roots	4 feet (1.2 meters)	active mostly at night	stay in mother's pouch for at least 6 months
Tasmanian Devil	Australia and Tasmania	small animals, dead animals	3–4 feet (.9–1.2 meters)	active mostly at night	stay in mother's pouch for at least 15 weeks
Kangaroo	deserts and grasslands of central Australia	grass, roots, and small plants	male: 6 feet (1.8 meters) female: 4.5 feet (1.4 meters)	active mostly at night or on cool days	stay in mother's pouch for 6–8 months
Platypus	streams (Australia)	shrimp, snails, insects, worms, crayfish	16–22 inches (41–56 centimeters)	active mostly at night	hatch from eggs after 10 days
Black Swan	lakes, ponds, and wet grass areas (Australia)	water plants	4 feet (1.2 meters)	active day and evening	hatch from eggs after 40 days
Dingo	Australia	dead animals, rabbits, wild pigs; sometimes kills and eats farm animals	2 feet tall (.6 meters), 3 feet long (.9 meters)	active mostly at night	born live in litter

Australia has some of the tallest trees in the world. These trees are part of the **eucalyptus** (you-kuh-LIP-tuhss) family. There are about 500 kinds of eucalyptus trees. Australians call small, shrub-like eucalyptuses "eucalypts," and tall, tree-like eucalyptuses "gum trees." The tallest eucalyptuses are mountain ash and karri trees. Mountain ash trees can grow to be more than 300 feet (91 meters) tall. About 100 years ago, eucalyptus trees were planted in America. Today they grow in several states, including California and Florida.

Australia also has **acacias** (uh-KAY-shuhz). Acacias are tropical trees that make a kind of gum that is used in many foods and medicines. Many acacias are small shrubs. There are more than 600 types of acacias in Australia. Small kinds have bright, beautiful flowers. Australians call acacias "wattles."

acacia tree

Here's a graph of some of the tallest trees that have ever grown in Australia.

eucalyptus trees

Tallest Australian Trees

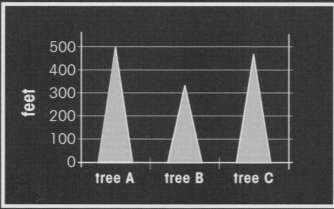

Tree A—(Victoria, Australia) Australian Eucalyptus: 492 feet (150 meters)
Tree B—(Tasmania, Australia) Australian Eucalyptus: 324.8 feet (99 meters)
Tree C—(Victoria, Australia) Australian Eucalyptus: 470 feet (143 meters)

Many fish and marine animals live in the waters off the coasts of Australia. The Great Barrier **Reef** is found along the northeastern coast of Australia. It is the world's largest reef. The Great Barrier Reef isn't really a single reef, but is actually made up of more than 2,500 coral reefs.

There are over 400 different kinds of coral that make up the reef. They come in many shapes and colors. About 1,500 different kinds of fish live around the Great Barrier Reef. Other sea creatures that live near the reef include giant clams, turtles, crabs, and many kinds of birds. People come from all over the world to explore this gigantic reef. The Great Barrier Reef measures about 1,400 miles (2,300 kilometers) long. The state of Texas is about 800 miles (1,287 kilometers) from top to bottom. That means the Great Barrier Reef is 600 miles (966 kilometers) longer than America's second largest state!

This pie chart shows information about Australian marine exports, or products sold to other countries. Prawns are animals that are like shrimp. Abalone are similar to snails. They can be eaten, and their shells—sometimes called mother-of-pearl—are used as decoration. Scallops are similar to clams and oysters.

clam

Great Barrier Reef

Australian Marine Exports

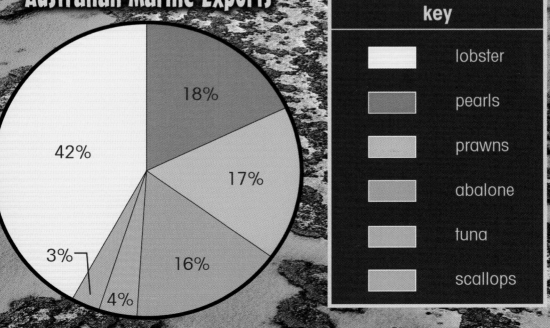

- 42%
- 18%
- 17%
- 16%
- 4%
- 3%

key

- lobster
- pearls
- prawns
- abalone
- tuna
- scallops

A Very Big Rock

Not only does Australia have the world's largest reef, it also has the world's largest single rock. The rock is called Ayers Rock, and it is famous. The Aborigines call it "Uluru," which means "great pebble." Uluru is a giant sandstone rock that is about 1.5 miles (2.4 kilometers) long. It is about 1,142 feet (348 meters) tall and more than 1 mile (1.6 kilometers) wide.

Aborigine **ancestors** painted pictures on the rock long ago. Today, Aborigines believe that Uluru is a very sacred place. The rock is on land that belongs to the Aborigines. However, the Australian government rents it from them so that everyone can go and see the wonder of Uluru.

Glossary

Aborigine (aa-buh-RIH-juh-nee) One of the native peoples of Australia who have lived there since long before anyone else arrived.

acacia (uh-KAY-shuh) A tree or shrub that has feathery leaves and flowers.

ancestor (AN-ses-tuhr) Someone in your family who lived before you.

column (KAH-luhm) A line of numbers or words running up and down a page.

commonwealth (KAH-muhn-welth) A federal union of states.

continent (KAHN-tuhn-uhnt) One of the 7 large landmasses on Earth.

equator (ih-KWAY-tuhr) An imaginary line around the middle of Earth, halfway between the North and South Poles.

eucalyptus (you-kuh-LIP-tuhss) A fragrant evergreen tree that grows mostly in Australia.

hemisphere (HEH-muh-sfeer) One-half of a planet.

plateau (pla-TOH) An area of high, flat land.

platypus (PLA-tih-puhs) An Australian mammal with webbed feet and a broad, soft bill that is a lot like a duck's bill.

reef (REEF) A chain of rocks or coral at or near the surface of a body of water.

transportation (transs-pur-TAY-shuhn) A means or system for moving people

Index

A
Aborigine(s), 12, 14, 22
animals, 16, 20
Australian Alps, 8
Ayers Rock, 22

C
Central Lowlands, 10
Cook, James, 12

D
desert(s), 8, 10

E
Eastern Highlands, 10

F
farmland(s), 10
forests, 10

G
grazing land, 10
Great Barrier Reef, 20

I
island continent, 6

J
Janszoon, William, 12

M
manufacturing, 10
mining, 10
mountain(s), 8, 10, 18

N
Northern Hemisphere, 4

O
outback, 14

S
Southern Hemisphere, 4

T
Tasmania, 6, 8
trees, 18

U
Uluru, 22

W
Western Plateau, 10

ML   6/04